Flying over the USA
Airplanes in American Life

Transportation
in America

Flying over the USA
Airplanes in American Life

Martin W. Sandler

OXFORD
UNIVERSITY PRESS

For Robbie, Winslow, Sarah, and Christopher. Like young people everywhere, their laughter and wisdom is all we know of magic.

OXFORD
UNIVERSITY PRESS

Oxford   New York
Auckland   Bangkok   Buenos Aires   Cape Town   Chennai
Dar es Salaam   Delhi   Hong Kong   Istanbul   Karachi   Kolkata
Kuala Lumpur   Madrid   Melbourne   Mexico City   Mumbai   Nairobi
São Paulo   Shanghai   Singapore   Taipei   Tokyo   Toronto

Published by Oxford University Press, Inc.
198 Madison Avenue, New York, New York 10016
www.oup.com

Oxford is a registered trademark of Oxford University Press

Library of Congress Cataloging-in-Publication Data
Sandler, Martin W.
  Flying over the USA : airplanes in American life / Martin W. Sandler.
      v. cm. -- (American transportation)
Includes bibliographical references and index.
Contents: Reaching for the sky—An age of heroes—Shrinking the nation—Transforming America—Change and challenge—Timeline—Places to visit.
   ISBN 0-19-513231-9 (alk. paper)
   1. Aeronautics—United States—History—Juvenile literature. 2. Airplanes—History—Juvenile literature. 3. Air travel—United States—History—Juvenile literature. [1. Aeronautics. 2. Airplanes—History. 3. Air travel.] I. Title. II. Series.
   TL547 .S323 2003
   629.13'0973—dc22   2003017876

Printing number: 9 8 7 6 5 4 3 2 1

Printed in Hong Kong on acid-free paper

Design by Alexis Siroc

ON THE COVER: **A 1949 Ryan Navion, which had a top speed of 157 miles per hour, takes off from an airport.**

FRONTISPIECE: **Biplanes perform a "follow-the-leader" routine for the crowds at the 1931 Cleveland National Air Races.**

Contents

CHAPTER 1

Reaching for the Sky

"With a short dash down the runway, the machine lifted into the air and was flying. It was only a flight of twelve seconds, and it was an uncertain, wavy, creeping sort of flight at best; but it was a real flight at last and not a glide."

—Orville Wright, in a telegram to his father
after completing the first successful manned, powered flight, 1903

"I sometimes think," said pioneer aviator Glenn Curtis in a speech to a flying club in 1907

> that the desire to fly after the fashion of the birds is an ideal handed down to us by our ancestors who in their grueling travels across trackless lands in prehistoric times, looked enviously on the birds soaring freely through space, at full speed, above all obstacles, on the infinite highway of the air.

The desire to fly may be as old as humanity itself. But it was not until the beginning of the 20th century that the first significant step in achieving powered, manned,

heavier-than-air flight (that is, not held aloft by a balloon full of light gas) took place.

In 1901, the American astronomer Samuel Pierpont Langley, inspired by European and American experiments with gliders and by the invention of the internal combustion engine, successfully flew a gas-powered model airplane. Two years later, Langley, who at the time was head of the Smithsonian Institution, built a full-size aircraft four times the size of his model.

On October 7, 1903, to much fanfare and in full view of the nation's press, Langley catapulted his plane, named the *Aerodrome,* from atop his houseboat anchored in the Potomac River. As the plane—piloted by Langley's colleague Charles Manley—took off, its wings suddenly collapsed, sending it crashing headfirst into the river. On December 8, Langley tried again. Once more the piloted *Aerodrome* catapulted forward, only to fall back almost immediately into the water, this time on its back.

Although Langley escaped serious injury, he became a laughingstock, heaped with ridicule rather than the acclaim for which he had hoped. His spectacular failures reinforced the convictions of those who continued to repeat the centuries-old adage that "If man had been meant to fly, he would have been given wings." More than ever, the general public was in agreement with

Long before serious would-be aviators like Samuel Langley and Wilbur and Orville Wright attempted flight, backyard builders made their own homemade inventions. The creator of this 1894 machine called it a "soaring aeroplane," but it literally never got off the ground.

astronomer and mathematician Simon Newcomb, who had asked, "May not our mechanicians...be ultimately forced to admit that aerial flight is one of the great class of problems with which man can never cope, and give up all attempts to grapple with it?" Yet only nine days after Samuel Langley's dream of glory ended in the Potomac, two bicycle-making brothers named Wilbur and Orville Wright would prove Newcomb and all the other critics wrong.

This was a remarkable time in the nation's history. Inventions in the field of transportation were profoundly changing the ways in which Americans worked, played, and lived. In 1888, when Orville was 17 and Wilbur was 21, the electric trolley was introduced. Less than a decade later, distances shrank even more as millions of people took to the roads in automobiles. This was called the Age of the Machine, and for the Wright brothers it was a most exciting time to be alive.

Even as youngsters, the Wright brothers had displayed a mechanical ability beyond their years. They inherited this talent from their mother, Sarah. Before she married, at a time when few women were involved in mechanical pursuits, Sarah Wright spent many hours tinkering with horse-drawn vehicles in her family's carriage business. In 1905, Wilbur and Orville's younger sister Katharine was quoted in the *Dayton Journal* as saying "Mother could make anything and make a good job of it. Wilbur and [Orville] got her genius in making things."

Their first business collaboration came when they formed a printing firm in Dayton, Ohio. In the 1890s they expanded their commercial interests by starting another company in Dayton that built, sold, and repaired bicycles. Bicycling had become a national craze, and the Wrights' cycling company was highly successful.

With each passing year, their interest in flight grew more intense. Then, in 1896, newspapers reported the death of the German aeronautical engineer Otto Lilienthal. The Wrights had closely followed reports of Lilienthal's experiments with gliders, and news of his

Samuel Langley's launching crew looks on as Langley's plane takes to the air. The unpiloted model plane was the largest and heaviest machine that had ever flown.

In the months leading up to their first powered flight, the Wright brothers made almost 1,000 glider flights on the windy slopes of Kill Devil Hills, North Carolina.

death inspired the brothers to make their own attempt to carry on Lilienthal's work.

The brothers began by reading everything they could find that had been written about previous flying experiments. They also began to correspond with such aeronautical pioneers as Samuel Langley. "I am an enthusiast, but not a crank..." Wilbur asserted in one of his letters to Langley. "I wish to avail myself of all that is already known and then if possible add my mite to help on the future worker who will attain final success."

Armed with what they had learned, the Wright brothers turned their full attention to making their own contributions to the achievement of manned, powered flight. They began by building a series of gliders. They knew that their first challenge would be to solve the control problem that all glider-makers had encountered— the very problem, in fact, that had caused Lilienthal's fatal crash. They first addressed this problem by developing "wing warping," a mechanical process by which they twisted the tips of their gliders' wings. They found that by constructing the wings in this fashion, they could keep their gliders from tipping sideways while in flight.

By 1900, the brothers were ready to test their gliders. For a testing site they chose a remote coastal spot in North Carolina called Kill Devil Hills, near the town of Kitty Hawk. "From the United States Weather Bureau reports," wrote Orville Wright in his book *How We Invented the Airplane,*

we found that Kitty Hawk was one of the windiest places in the country, and that during the month of September it had average winds in the neighborhood of 16 miles an hour. We wrote to the weather bureau man at the Kitty Hawk station, telling him of the nature of the experiments we wished to conduct and asking him in regard to the suitability of the ground in that neighborhood. We received a very favorable report from him, and also from the postmaster at Kitty Hawk, to whom he had shown our letter.

Convinced that the Kitty Hawk area, with its high and constant winds, was a perfect site for their glider experiments, the Wrights built a shack in the sand dunes there. They set up house in this shack for the summer, and also built several long sheds to house their gliders and their tools and other equipment.

At first they conducted their tests by piloting the gliders. But when Orville was injured in a spinout, they decided that it was more prudent to conduct these initial experiments with an unmanned full-sized craft. In the next weeks they were able to keep the glider aloft far longer than Lilienthal or any other experimenters had ever managed. Despite these record-making unmanned flights, however, the tests were not a complete success. The Wrights still had difficulty controlling the movements of their aircraft.

When cold weather set in, the Wrights returned to Dayton. But the next summer they were back at Kill Devil Hills with a much bigger glider. The summer of 1901 turned out to be a season of frustration and discouragement. At first the glider delivered much less lift than the brothers expected. After they found a way to give the glider more lift, they found that the aircraft was still too difficult to control. The brothers made adjustments, but these alterations caused the lift problem to return. Stormy weather, which limited the number of flights the brothers could conduct, made matters worse.

It was the low point in the Wrights' aviation career. "We doubted that we would ever resume our experiments," wrote Wilbur in his book *How We Invented the Airplane*.

Although we had broken the record for distance in gliding, . . . we looked at the time and money which we had expended . . . and the distance yet to go, and we considered our experiments a failure. At that time I made the prediction that men would sometime fly, but that it would not be within our lifetime.

Fortunately, another winter back in Dayton rekindled the brothers' determination to succeed. There they built a wind tunnel, which helped them refine their knowledge of the way air moves over a wing. Most important, they finally hit upon a device that would at last solve the control problem that they and all previous flyers had encountered. They discovered that by adding a tail to the rear of the aircraft they could gain full control over it. They coupled this breakthrough with another discovery: linking a glider's rudder to the wings eliminated the spinouts that often occurred when a glider pilot tried to make a turn.

In the summer of 1902 the brothers returned to Kill Devil Hills, where they made more than 50 successful test flights. With the aid of their bicycle shop's

By inventing this propeller shaped like a twisted wing, the Wright brothers found a way to give their plane enough thrust to keep it in the air.

mechanic, Charles Taylor, they had built a light 12-horsepower gasoline engine and had installed it in their plane. Their final innovation was a new type of propeller, which was shaped like a twisted wing. This gave the aircraft considerably more thrust.

After successfully testing the new tail, rudder, engine, and propeller throughout the summer and well into the fall of 1903, the Wrights were ready for a series of powered flights that they hoped would propel them into history. They made their first attempt in their airplane, named the *Flyer,* on December 14. They flipped a coin to determine who would be at the controls, and Wilbur won. The wind, however, was very light, and the *Flyer* stalled on takeoff, hitting the ground and damaging the rudder. Three days later, after making the necessary repairs, they were ready to try again.

December 17, 1903, dawned gray, with cold, blustery winds. The Wrights warmed themselves by a small stove in their shack as they waited for the winds to calm down. By 10:00 AM it became clear that the weather was not going to improve, but the brothers decided to risk going ahead with the test.

Orville and Wilbur began their test by raising a signal banner. It was a way of letting the men at the nearby Kill Devil Hills Life Saving Station know they were about to begin a flight. It was also a prearranged way of inviting them to witness the test. The brothers then laid down the 60-foot wooden rail from which they would launch the *Flyer.*

THE DAYTON JOURNAL.

ORVILLE WRIGHT CONQUERS AIR IN AMAZING FLIGHT

Years of Scientific Research Crowned by Dayton Man in Record-Breaking Test.

FLYING IS NOW CONCEDED AS AN ESTABLISHED FACT

Cruises in Invisible Currents of Ether Now a Certainty and Darius Green's Dream Is Made a Living Reality.

Orville Wright a volé hier pendant presque une heure

TOUS LES RECORDS D'AVIATION SONT BATTUS

Orville and Wilbur were equally responsible for the achievement of manned, powered flight. Wilbur Wright may have made the longest flight of the day, but it was Orville who made the first one and, as the front page of the *Dayton Journal* reveals, received more acclaim.

Next the Wrights poured gasoline into the engine, placed a battery on one of the wings, and hooked its wires to the engine. Then they started the engine. Finally, Orville climbed onto the plane and lay down flat on the lower wing, next to the engine. After checking the controls, he was ready.

At 10:35 AM Orville released the wires that held the aircraft to the launching rail. The *Flyer* made its way down the track with Wilbur running alongside it to balance the wing. As the airplane approached the end of the rails, Wilbur let go and the *Flyer* lifted into the air. Twelve seconds later, after flying unevenly, it came down 120 feet from where the flight had begun. A few minutes later, Wilbur took the controls and flew 195 feet. Orville tried again and accomplished a 200-foot flight. On the last flight of the day, Wilbur stayed aloft for 59 seconds and flew 852 feet.

Shortly after Wilbur completed the fourth and final flight, a huge gust of wind caught hold of the airplane and flipped it end over end. The wings and the engine were so badly damaged that the *Flyer* would never be sent aloft again. But the brothers had done it. The goal of manned, powered, heavier-than-air flight—for which so many had struggled and more than a few had died—had been attained. A young boy who witnessed the achievement perhaps put it best. As he raced toward the town of Kitty Hawk to spread the news he shouted, "They done it! They done it! Damned if they ain't flew."

The Wright brothers had flown, alright. And when, in the two years following their triumph, they built two more-advanced planes and flew them before huge crowds in Europe and the United States, even the greatest skeptics became convinced that the world had entered the Age of Flight. This was particularly true in the United States, where, beginning in 1910, the public across the country was introduced to flying through spectacular flying exhibitions.

These demonstrations were carried out by daring aviators who earned their living by touring the nation and performing death-defying aerial feats. These stunt fliers were nicknamed "barnstormers" because many of their

A daredevil hangs from a rope ladder while his plane is in full flight. Such brave men and women introduced a skeptical public to the thrills of flying.

Harriet Quimby climbs aboard her Blériot biplane. One of the most daring of all pioneer pilots, Quimby, like many early aviators, died in a plane crash.

stunts were performed above cow pastures, and many of the pilots ended their day by sleeping in the barns above which they had flown.

Appearing before crowds at country fairs, racetracks, and almost any other open area where they could attract a throng, these daredevils continually invented new and amazing tricks. They hung upside down from one of their plane's wings. They climbed from one airplane to another while in full flight. They played a mock game of tennis standing on the wings while flying at top speeds. A favorite stunt was to terrify spectators by power-diving to within a few feet of the ground before straightening out and landing in front of a grandstand. In their calmer moments barnstormers gave people their first ride in an airplane, charging from $2 to $25, depending on the length of the flight.

Because of their breathtaking antics, the stunt fliers were often described by the newspapers of the day as "the amazing young men in their flying machines." But this was inaccurate, for several of the daredevils— Blanche Scott, Harriet Quimby, Ruth Law, and Katherine Stinson—were women. These women not only thrilled crowds with their aerial feats, but also set several speed and altitude records in the process. At a time when many people believed that women could not compete successfully with men in most fields, these daring and skilled aviators dramatically proved that those who held this belief were dead wrong.

CHAPTER 2

An Age of Heroes

"My eyes feel hard and dry as stones. The lids pull down with pounds of weight against the muscles."

—Charles Lindbergh, describing in his journal how he felt while
battling to stay awake during his solo flight across the Atlantic, 1927

With their spectacular exhibitions, stunt fliers not only introduced Americans to the possibilities of flight, but also set the stage for another type of activity that drew even greater crowds and attention to the world of aviation. This was the air meet, a highly organized event in which pilots from around the world competed in a variety of events for large cash prizes. The most popular of the many air meets held in the United States were the Belmont Races, held in New York State; the Pulitzer Race, staged in St. Louis; the Bendix Races, flown between Los Angeles and Cleveland; and the cross-country Women's Air Derby.

While these aerial competitions were capturing the nation's attention, another development in flying was taking place, one that, though not as thrilling as the air races, would have a much greater impact on the lives of the American public. At a time when much of the nation was still without telephone service, and such advancements as faxes and computers were a long way off, mail was the primary form of long-distance communication. Beginning with the Pony Express and through to the delivery of letters and packages by train and truck, people had been searching for new and

The 1931 National Air Races took place during an entire week and featured a variety of competitions, including a women's air derby in which pilots competed in speed and distance contests.

1931 NATIONAL AIR RACES
CLEVELAND

OFFICIAL PROGRAM
PRICE 25¢

speedier ways of delivering of the mail. By the second decade of the 1900s it became clear that the airplane presented the fastest means of all.

The first airmail flight in the United States began from a field in Washington, D.C., on May 15, 1918. As thousands of spectators, including President Woodrow Wilson, looked on, an airplane was loaded with 140 pounds of mail to be delivered to New York City. It was hardly a glorious beginning. Try as he might, the Army pilot commissioned for the task could not get the plane to start. Then someone noticed that the fuel tank was empty. Finally, with the gas tank duly filled, the pilot took off—and headed in the wrong direction. It did not take him long to realize that he was lost, so he put down in a field somewhere in Maryland. What should have been the nation's first load of airmail was then transferred to a train heading for New York.

By August of that year, the United States Post Office had officially taken over airmail service, and things began to go more smoothly. Within a year, the post office had made more than 1,200 flights, most in the eastern part of the nation. By 1920, airmail service had been extended from the East Coast to Omaha, Nebraska. But there was a drawback: None of the airfields used by the airmail pilots was equipped with lights or flashing beacons. Trains were still needed to move the mail at night.

In February 1921, the post office achieved a milestone when it flew mail from San Francisco to New York City for the first time. The time needed to deliver mail from coast to coast had been reduced from 108 hours by train to 33 hours by air. It was a breakthrough that so impressed President Warren Harding that he agreed to support the post office's request to install lights and beacons at all landing fields used by airmail pilots.

The lighting of airfields was a major step forward, but flying the mail was still a very hazardous undertaking. As a rookie airmail pilot Ralph Wilson wrote in a letter to his daughter in 1923, "You can't imagine what it is to fly in an open cockpit, never knowing what type of weather is ahead or whether the engine is going to quit. But it's sure teaching me to fly."

Learn to fly they did, and throughout the first two decades of the 1900s pilots set records in almost every area of aviation. But one great goal still remained—that of making a solo, nonstop flight across the Atlantic. In 1919 two British aviators, John Alcock and Arthur Whitten Brown, had earned a £10,000 (about $17,000) prize by flying from Newfoundland, Canada, to Ireland, but no one had done it alone.

When in 1926 another prize, this one for $25,000, was offered by the wealthy hotelier Raymond Orteig for the first nonstop, solo flight between New York City and Paris, interest in an Atlantic crossing was rekindled. Among those who became determined to win the award was a tall, shy 25-year-old from Detroit named Charles

The sign on the plane reads: FIRST AIR MAIL TO Germany FROM Chicago

✈ Flying over the USA

Lindbergh. A former barnstormer and one of the nation's first airmail pilots, Lindbergh persuaded a group of St. Louis businessmen to put up the $10,000 necessary to build an airplane in which he could make his attempt. He then had Ryan Airlines of San Diego build the aircraft.

Lindbergh named the airplane *Spirit of St. Louis* in honor of the city in which he had raised his funds. While it was being constructed, he devoted his time to planning the flight. He knew that it would be important to keep the airplane as light as possible. He was also concerned about whether or not the amount of fuel the plane could carry would be enough to get him across the Atlantic. For food, he decided to take only five cans of military rations. "If I get to Paris," he told reporters, "I won't need any more. And if I don't get to Paris, I won't need any more either."

The sign on the plane in this 1921 photograph boasted that it was making the first airmail delivery to Europe. In fact, the mail was flown from around the United States to the East Coast, where it was then loaded onto ships and transported across the Atlantic.

Two months after the Ryan company had begun construction, the *Spirit of St. Louis* was ready. Lindbergh knew that he was hardly the only one who was going after the prize. But he was also aware that those who had tried before him had met with disaster. A French crew of five had crashed when a gear on their plane had collapsed, and American pilot Richard Byrd had also crashed during a test flight. And on May 8 a crew led by the French air ace Charles Nungesser, attempting to make the flight in the opposite direction from Lindbergh's attempt (Paris to New York), had disappeared into the Atlantic.

On May 20, with these sobering facts in mind, and while ships in the North Atlantic were still looking for Nungesser and his crew (they were never found), Lindbergh, took off from Roosevelt Field on Long Island, New York. In his tiny airplane, equipped with only a compass for navigation, he headed for Paris. Because of the extra fuel tanks he had ordered installed in the front of his enclosed cockpit, his forward vision was completely blocked and he had to use a periscope

The Short Life of Airships

Some of the first airlines did not transport their passengers on airplanes, but in a different kind of aircraft: the cigar-shaped dirigible, or airship, as it was called. Powered by hydrogen, the dirigible was a descendant of the hot-air and hydrogen balloons that had first launched men and women into the air.

The most famous commercial dirigible was the huge German ship *Hindenburg,* which provided up to 50 passengers with amenities that rivaled the world's finest hotels. Meals aboard the airship were even more sumptuous and elegant than those served on the most lavish ocean liners. By 1937, the *Hindenburg* had earned such a reputation as the epitome of luxury travel that 18 transatlantic flights had been scheduled for that year and extra cabins had been built to accommodate more passengers. But on May 6, 1937, with a crowd of spectators, newspaper reporters, and photographers looking on, the *Hindenburg* suddenly burst into flames as it approached its mooring at Lakehurst, New Jersey. The *Hindenburg* disaster marked the end of the glory days of the dirigible. From that time on, it would be airplanes, not airships, that would carry passengers in ever-increasing numbers to places throughout the world.

The explosion of the *Hindenburg* became one of the most publicized of all early aviation disasters, thanks to dramatic pictures such as this one.

to see anything in front of the aircraft. The takeoff itself was nerve-wracking. Buffeted by bad weather, the airplane fought to get into the air. *The Spirit of St. Louis,*" Lindbergh wrote in his log, "feels more like an overloaded truck than an airplane."

Aside from his twin concerns about having enough fuel and finding his way, the young pilot knew that the greatest challenge of flying for the more than 33 hours that the flight would require was to keep himself awake. Midway through his journey he wrote, "My eyes feel dry and hard as stones. The lids pull down with pounds of weight against the muscles." Lindbergh began to use his cupped hands to direct the icy wind that entered the cockpit toward his face, hoping that this would help keep him from falling asleep. Sometime during the night portion of his trip, he resorted to holding his eyelids open with his thumbs to keep from dozing off.

During the long night and through the clouds and fog that continually surrounded him, Lindbergh found himself flying as though blind. In another log entry he wrote, "Everything is uniform blackness except for the exhaust's flash on passing mist and the glowing dials in my cockpit, so different from all other lights. My world and my life are compressed within these walls."

When dawn finally came Lindbergh looked out and saw that the clouds had broken. In the 26th hour of his flight he spotted first a porpoise, then some birds, and finally some boats. Then he crossed over land so green that he knew it had to be Ireland. The excitement of realizing where he was filled his bone-weary body with new energy.

Seven hours later he reached the outskirts of Paris. When he touched down at Le Bourget airfield, a jubilant French crowd, having been alerted by radio from Ireland, pulled him out of his cockpit and carried him off in triumph. The reaction in the United States was even more ecstatic. "When I heard on the radio what Lindbergh had done, I was so proud to be an American," Selma Krames, then a teenager, later recalled. "His achievement," proclaimed the editor of the *New Bedford Standard Times,* "shows the world what can be done

The cockpit of the *Spirit of St. Louis* was so cramped that there was barely enough room for Charles Lindbergh to sit at the controls during his solo flight across the Atlantic Ocean.

Charles Lindbergh (far right) pays a visit to Orville Wright (far left) and Major John F. Curry at Wright Field in Dayton, Ohio, in 1927, barely one month after his historic transatlantic flight.

with courage and belief in one's self. Let us hope that upon his return, young Lindbergh is given a hero's welcome unlike any we have ever witnessed." The editor was not disappointed. After being honored in Europe, Lindbergh returned to the United States on a Navy ship sent by President Calvin Coolidge. When he reached New York City, some four million people lined the streets for the ticker-tape parade.

Charles Lindbergh had become the greatest aviation hero of all. But the age of heroes of flight was not over. In 1928, little more than a year after Lindbergh's historic achievement, Amelia Earhart, who was to become the most famous female pilot, was the first woman to fly across the Atlantic. She was a passenger on that flight, but in 1932 she found herself an international hero when she became the first woman to accomplish the feat alone.

Honors of all kinds were heaped upon Earhart, including the National Geographic's Special Gold Medal. When a French newspaper ended an article about all her awards with the words "[but] can she bake a cake?"

Earhart made a pointed reply. "I accept these awards," she stated, "on behalf of the cake bakers and all those other women who can do some things quite as important, if not more important, than flying, as well as in the name of women flying today."

During this period, former stunt flier Wiley Post also set notable records. In 1931, accompanied by a navigator, he flew around the globe in 8 days and 15 hours. Two years later, in what many at the time regarded as the greatest flying feat of all, Post flew around the world again, in just 7 days and 19 hours—and this time he did it alone.

Just as the Wright brothers' flight had ushered in an age of daredevils and barnstormers who introduced Americans to flying, the accomplishments of Wiley Post, Amelia Earhart, and Charles Lindbergh bolstered the public's confidence in the possibilities of travel by air. Soon the airplane would change people's lives in ways that even the most optimistic early champions of flight could hardly have imagined.

Amelia Earhart stands in front of the Lockheed 10E Electra airplane in which she attempted her around-the-world flight in 1937.

CHAPTER 3

Shrinking the Nation

"This is the most important aviation development since Lindbergh's flight.

In one fell swoop, we have shrunk the earth."

—Juan Trippe, founder of Pan American Airlines, in a speech about the jet engine, 1947

The achievements in aviation during the first two decades of the 20th century took place so quickly that by the late 1920s, when the first popular passenger airlines were established, it was difficult to believe that it had only been 25 years since the Wright brothers' epic flight. At the heart of the rise of the passenger airlines were the technological breakthroughs, including the introduction of new materials such as aluminum, which made it possible to build much larger aircraft. The advancements brought about because of airmail service, such as well-lighted airfields, also paved the way for passenger airlines. Two other factors—the training of American military pilots during World War I and the formation of the National Air Pilots Association in 1928—helped set the stage for the beginning of widespread commercial flight.

The first passenger airlines had actually begun operations in Europe years before, in 1919. Development of passenger lines in the United States was slower because the early American airlines found that they could make much more money by getting government contracts to carry the mail than they could by transporting travelers. The earliest airlines that did accept passengers made them sign a release stating that they would leave the plane at any landing site along the route if the airline was given more mail bags to take their place.

In the middle of the 1920s, however, things began to change for the airlines. It was now possible to build much larger airplanes, which allowed airlines to turn a profit by carrying many more passengers in a single flight than ever before. Equally important, planes were becoming much safer, which boosted public confidence in air travel.

Gone were the open cockpits, replaced by pilots' cabins. The new technologies of radio direction-finding and voice communications had improved air navigation skills immeasurably. Seat belts, which had been introduced in airmail flights, were now standard equipment for passengers. Added to all these improvements were the many airline mergers that took place. Smaller airlines combined their resources into large companies, which, along with making the new companies profitable, made them considerably more efficient.

As the 1930s approached, the United States could boast of a number of major airlines, including Trans World Airlines, American Airlines, United Airlines, and Eastern Airlines. It was Pan American Airlines, however, that enjoyed the greatest success early on.

This cut-away model of the 1939 model Boeing 314 Clipper reveals seven passenger sections, including a first class compartment called the "De Luxe Suite" at the rear of the plane.

After starting its passenger business in 1929, Pan Am, as it was called, began to fly many of its routes not with airliners as we know them today, but huge aircraft known as flying boats or clippers. The fuselage (main body) of a clipper was designed like the hull of a boat. Major airports and runways were still scarce in the 1930s, so the flying boats' ability to land in harbors and seaports gave them a distinct advantage over the airliners that had to set down on land.

The fleet of so-called Clippers that Pan American launched in the 1930s enabled the company to expand its air routes around the world. Many of the aircraft had wood-paneled walls, silk drapery, and upholstered seats and sleeper cabins.

The world's first stewardesses, who were required to be registered nurses, pose beside a 1930s airliner.

The luxurious features of Pan American's Flying Clippers inspired many of the airline's competitors to provide similar comforts. This 1940 brochure advertising TWA's fleet of Boeing 307 Stratoliners illustrates the planes' spacious passenger compartments.

The most impressive of these flying boats were the China Clippers, which carried passengers across both the Atlantic and Pacific oceans at cruising speeds of more than 170 miles per hour (as compared to the 70-mile-per-hour speed of the first airmail flights).

As flights operated by airlines such as Pan American became safer and more efficient, they also became more passenger-friendly. In 1930, for example, Ellen Church, a 26-year-old registered nurse who also held a pilot's license, approached executives of Boeing Air Transport with a novel idea. Church proposed that Boeing hire registered nurses like herself to be included as part of passenger-flight crews. These women, she told the executives, could take care of any passengers who happened to get sick, and could also tend to their other needs.

The executives liked the idea and hired Church and seven other nurses for a three-month trial period. Passengers responded so positively to the women's services that Boeing soon hired more women, dropping the requirement that they be nurses. Other airlines soon followed suit, and stewardesses, as they came be called, became an integral part of the airline industry.

Pan American's Flying Clippers were the largest commercial planes of their time. The *Honolulu Clipper* in this travel poster lands on the water and passengers exit onto a dock, two reasons the clippers were nicknamed flying boats.

HAWAII BY FLYING CLIPPER

HONOLULU CLIPPER

PAA

PAN AMERICAN AIRWAYS SYSTEM

In 1926, airlines in the United States carried about 6,000 passengers. By 1941, almost three million people traveled by air annually. The airliners that appeared in the early 1940s offered passengers more safety and speed than any aircraft previously built. Capable of cruising at speeds in excess of 250 miles per hour, they featured air-cooled engines, retractable landing gear, split wing flaps, and pressurized cabins.

Many types of these airliners were built, but one particular model stood head and shoulders above the rest. It was the Douglas Corporation's DC-3. Extremely safe and efficient, the DC-3 became the most popular airplane in the world. It was so popular, in fact, that by the early 1940s DC-3s were transporting 90 percent of the world's air travelers.

Thanks in great measure to the DC-3, the airliner had become a major factor in business and social lives around the world. Businesspeople increasingly discovered that traveling by air to meet with current or potential customers or to attend important meetings saved precious time and gave them the personal contact that neither the mail nor the telephone could provide. Families discovered that they could visit distant relatives or take a vacation in a faraway place much more easily than ever before.

The airliners of the early and mid-1940s were the most visible reminders of the advancements made in aviation. But ahead lay even more spectacular developments. One of these took place on October 19, 1947. On that day, the American test pilot Charles "Chuck" E. Yeager, flying in a bullet-nosed, rocket-powered research airplane, became the first human to fly faster than what is known as Mach 1, the speed of sound. Yeager's achievement was the beginning of a whole new era of flight. In a single year—1953—Yeager would set yet another speed record, reaching Mach 2.44 (1,650 miles per hour); and U.S. Marine Corps pilot Marion J. Carl would set a new altitude mark at 82,235 feet.

As these records were broken, the entire airline industry continued to see changes. In 1945, airlines throughout the world transported some 9,300,000 people. To many observers it seemed that the ultimate

Chuck Yeager sits in the cockpit of his rocket-powered plane, the *Glamorous Glennis,* which was named after his wife. After breaking the sound barrier he became known as "the fastest man alive."

travel faster, higher, and for greater distances than previously thought possible.

The first jet aircraft engines (engines driven by a powerful discharge of air rather than by pistons) were developed in the late 1940s, largely as the result of technological breakthroughs made by both American and British aviation experts during World War II. In May 1952, a British Overseas Aircraft Company (BOAC) fleet of aircraft named Comets became the world's first jetliners. Capable of flying eight miles up into the stratosphere and thus above most weather systems, the Comets

in air travel had been achieved. But those who believed this were forgetting that aviation, from its beginnings, had been characterized by one rapid technological advancement after another. By 1952, a whole new type of power source, the jet engine, would enable airliners to provided passengers with the smoothest ride airline travelers had yet experienced. But within two years disaster struck.

In 1954, two Comets disappeared while in flight over the Atlantic Ocean. All that was found of each plane was wreckage floating on the water. Intense investigation pinpointed the cause of both tragedies as metal fatigue in the body of the aircraft. The wear was caused by repeated takeoffs and landings at extremely high speed. The entire fleet of Comets was immediately and permanently grounded.

By the end of the 1950s, however, the mechanical problems that had doomed the Comets had been identified and solved, and airlines throughout the world began using jetliners. "For the first time I was flying by jet propulsion," exclaimed pilot Adolph Galland, one of the first American pilots to captain a jetliner. "No engine vibrations. No . . . lashing sound of the propeller. Accompanied by a whistling sound, [the plane] shot through the air. Later, when asked what it felt like, I said 'it felt as though angels were pushing.'"

The impact of the jet on the flying public was just as pronounced. "I'll never forget the first business trips I took by jetliner," recalled Robert Downing, an investment broker just out of college, in a 1959 issue of the United Airlines company magazine.

> I started the day with a breakfast meeting in Boston, and then met with clients over lunch in Chicago. I then caught a jetliner to Los Angeles where, early that evening, I met with some other customers. Later that night I was winging my way back to Boston. It was while I was flying home that it really struck me how much the jet airplane was going to change not only the way I would be conducting business but the whole new way in which business and industry in general would be operating.

Downing also remembers another first-time experience connected with his initial flights by jetliner. It never struck me," he says,

> that I would be flying through such different time zones in a single day. When I landed back in Boston my watch was still set on Los Angeles

One of Pan American's fleet of Boeing 377 Stratocruisers flies above the clouds. One of the most luxurious planes of its time, the Stratocruiser was known as the "First Lady of the Airways."

time. It read 11 PM but that was 2 AM Boston time. By the time I got home to bed it was 3 AM and believe me, I felt it the next day.

The physical effects that Downing had experienced were what most long-distance jet travelers still encounter. Today we call it jet lag.

Businessmen like Robert Downing were far from the only ones in the late 1950s and 1960s who experienced changes and were presented with new opportunities by jet travel. People wealthy enough to afford the price of flying by jetliner eventually discovered that they could leave work early on a Friday evening, jet off to places like Paris or the Caribbean for the weekend, and then jet back home in time for the beginning of the new work week. A whole new type of social activity was born. It was called "jet-setting," and it attracted those seeking to gain social status by demonstrating that they had the means to jet off whenever they wanted, to wherever they wished.

Jet-propelled aircraft not only changed the speed with which passengers could be transported to their

During the 1950s and 60s, airlines decorated objects such as timetables, napkins, and coasters with colorful illustrations. This Pan American-Grace Airways luggage tag reminded travelers that the airline served several cities in South America.

destinations, but also had a significant impact on the airfreight industry. Because airplanes, no matter how large, cannot carry as much cargo overseas as a ship or as much freight domestically as a train, it is not the quantity of goods they carry but the speed with which they can deliver goods that is the key to making airfreight a successful venture.

Vertical Flight

In the 1950s, while jet airliners were making their initial appearance, a totally different kind of aircraft also came onto the aviation scene: the helicopter. Featuring rotary blades on its top rather than wings and propellers or jet engines, its main advantage remains its ability to take off and land vertically in a minimum amount of space and without a runway.

The idea of the helicopter is far from new. The concept was first mentioned in a fourth-century Chinese book. In 1490 the Italian artist and inventor Leonardo da Vinci took the concept further when he sketched what he called the "helical air screw." It was not until the late 1930s, however, that the first truly workable helicopter was perfected in the United States by a Russian immigrant, Igor Sikorsky.

Since then, helicopters have become almost indispensable in many areas of life. Because of their ability to take off and land in even the most remote areas, they have become an important military weapon. They also often provide the fastest and most effective means of transporting accident and disaster victims to hospitals. And affluent travelers throughout the world avoid long and congested treks between airports and their urban destinations by making the trip by helicopter.

This helicopter delivers equipment and supplies to a research site where a landing strip for airplanes is unavailable.

CHAPTER 4

Airplanes at Work

"There is a real need and market for a company that will pick up small packages in one part of the country and deliver them efficiently and without hitches to another in a short period of time."

—Fred Smith, founder of Federal Express, in a speech to investors, 1972

As early as 1910, only seven years after the Wright brothers' first flight, some aviation visionaries began predicting that, given the unprecedented speed of aircraft, the airplane would soon become a major carrier of freight. It was in 1910, in fact, that the first practical demonstration of airfreight took place. In November of that year, an Ohio department store shipped a bolt of silk from Dayton to Columbus by air. The fact that the shipment arrived some two hours sooner than if it had been carried by train was deemed noteworthy enough that several Ohio newspapers reported the event.

During the 1920s, as airplanes grew larger, the amount of freight shipped by air grew significantly. In 1927, for example, only about 48,500 pounds of goods were shipped by air. By 1929 this figure had grown to some 258,00 pounds, and by 1932 to more than 1 million pounds. Most of the cargo was carried by new airfreight companies such as National Air Transport and General Air Express. The largest carrier of airfreight by far during this early period was automotive pioneer Henry Ford's express company, created specifically to carry automotive parts and other supplies to the

various Ford automobile-manufacturing plants around the country. Between 1925 and 1929, this company carried an average of 3 million pounds of automotive freight a year.

As promising as these early figures were, however, during the 1930s and 1940s air freight failed to live up to the expectations of its promoters. The main reason was that most of the major companies carrying freight at this time were companies that earned most of their money transporting passengers. As passenger revenues continued to rise, most of these companies began to concentrate exclusively on passenger service.

A plane drops its fire-dousing load over a blazing forest. The need to get as close to the fire as possible in spite of the turbulence caused by the intense heat makes piloting these planes a difficult task.

There was, however, one notable exception. In January 1946, Robert Prescott, who had been a pilot in the "Flying Tigers" squadron in World War II, founded Flying Tiger Line. Unlike the owners of previous freight companies, Prescott realized that in order to achieve success in his industry he would need to attract as diversified a group of customers as he could. Using his military, government, and business contacts, he did just that, and, by the end of its first year of operation, Flying Tiger Line had pilots flying coast-to-coast carrying freight.

Prescott also added to the line's revenues by signing cooperative agreements with railroad companies to deliver their freight from the airport to the railroad terminals. By the middle of the 1960s, Flying Tiger Line was making a yearly profit of $20 million and had established itself as the largest cargo airline in the United States.

A smokejumper parachutes into a fire zone that can be reached only by air. Once on the ground he will battle the blaze with equipment parachuted into the area by other planes.

By the 1960s the airplane had not only changed the way people traveled, but had also profoundly improved the way many jobs were carried out and the quality of services that the public received. Thanks to the airplane, for example, news reporting became more immediate and more accurate. Whenever a major event took place, no matter where in the world, reporters and photographers could fly to the scene and provide the public with eyewitness accounts of what was taking place.

The airplane also changed how disasters were handled. Wherever a calamity took place, be it an earthquake, a flood, a tornado, a drought, or a forest fire, relief workers could be flown immediately to the site to bring aid and comfort to the victims. Cargo planes could be used to transport food, clothing, and medical supplies to those suddenly in need.

In addition to bringing relief, airplanes also became a major tool for dealing with certain types of disasters while they were taking place. Those engaged in fighting forest fires, for example, discovered that huge amounts of water dropped from specially equipped planes could be highly effective in battling a blaze.

Farmers also benefited from the increased sophistication and maneuverability of aircraft. From the days of the pioneers who had filled the prairies with crops, one of the greatest challenges farmers faced was the threat of their plants being destroyed by insects. Increasingly, farmers began employing highly skilled pilots who, in planes capable of flying close to the ground (called crop dusters), were able to cover thousands of acres with insect-killing spray in a single day.

By the 1960s, aerial photography had advanced far beyond the point of novelty. The practice was not new: The first photographs taken from the air were taken from the baskets of hot air balloons. But now, thanks to improvements both in aircraft and in photographic equipment, pictures could be taken from the air that were not only of the highest quality but were useful to people in numerous ways. Mapmakers, for instance, could now use pictures of huge areas taken from high above the earth to aid them in producing

A crop duster makes a pass at an Iowa cornfield. When spraying fields with pesticide, pilots often fly at altitudes of less than 15 feet.

accurate maps. City and town planners found that aerial photographs of their communities helped them in laying out new streets and roads and in planning for both the expansion and the addition of new public utilities and other services. Pictures taken from aircraft also armed environmentalists with an important weapon in their fight to protect nature and natural resources. Aerial photographs provided concrete evidence of areas threatened by the carelessness of humans.

The airplane also benefited people everywhere by making the always difficult task of weather forecasting easier. As planes became capable of flying higher and farther, they were used to track approaching storms, even those hundreds of miles away.

The experience of air travel was changed yet again in 1969 by an influential development in the airline industry. That year, Boeing Corporation introduced the 747, the world's first so-called wide-body airliner, also known as a jumbo jet. The 350-ton 747 was about 19 1/2 feet wide and its body was almost as long as a football field. The tail of the plane was as tall as a six-story building.

The size of the mammoth jetliner made it capable of carrying several hundred passengers. By packing so many travelers into each aircraft, airlines using jumbo jets could slash air fares while at the same time reducing the number of aircraft they needed to remain competitive. The success of the 747 led other aircraft makers to begin producing their own wide-bodies. In 1970, a group of major European aircraft companies introduced the Airbus. Other manufacturers such as Lockheed and McDonnell Douglas soon followed suit, and by the end of the 1970s jumbo jets had become a staple of the airline industry.

The development of the jumbo jet benefited not only the airline companies, but also the passengers they

Aerial photography has improved the accuracy of weather forecasting in general and the tracking of severe storms in particular. This weather plane from the National Oceanic and Atmospheric Administration is carrying state-of-the-art photographic, forecasting, and communications equipment as it flies into the eye of a hurricane, where it will immediately relay such information as the size of the storm, its speed, and the direction in which it is most likely to travel.

carried. Using the wide-bodies, particularly the Airbus A310, several airlines established hourly shuttle service on busy routes such as those between Boston and New York, Washington and New York, and Los Angeles and San Francisco. Both business travelers and pleasure-seekers discovered that these places were now as accessible to them by shuttle flight as their nearest towns were by automobile.

Passenger airlines continued to grow throughout the 1960s and early 1970s. At the same time, however, freight remained a small part of total air traffic. That all changed in 1973, when a young entrepreneur named Fred Smith transformed the nature of the airfreight business. Smith believed that combining passenger service with airfreight delivery was a most inefficient way of doing business. The two types of service, he stated, require totally different routes. Besides, he also knew that meeting the demands of passengers slows down cargo delivery.

Smith had other important insights as well. He realized that one of the major inefficiencies of the air-freight business was the fact that few packages were sent directly to their destinations by existing carriers such as the post office, Railway Express, or Flying Tiger. Instead, packages were, as he put it, "hippity-hopping around the country from city to city and from airline to airline before reaching their destination."

Smith was also more aware than most of the changing nature of American business. "The new society that is building up our economy," he proclaimed in 1974,

> is no longer built around automobile and steel production, but is built up instead around service industries and high technology endeavors in electronics and optics and medical science. There is a real need and market for a company that can pick up small packages in one part of the country and deliver them efficiently and without hitches to another in a short period of time. I am convinced that customers will be willing to pay premium rates for such assured deliveries.

Based on these convictions, Smith established a company in Memphis, Tennessee, whose sole purpose would be airfreight delivery. He named his company

Federal Express, and he launched it with an unprecedented promise to the public. Federal Express, through the use of jumbo jets and other aircraft, would guarantee next-day delivery of packages.

After just three years in business, Federal Express was showing a profit. By 1982 the company had more than 76 aircraft, including 45 jumbo jets. In 1983, revenues rose to $1 billion, a record-breaking sum for a company only 10 years old. In 1989, Federal Express added to

its clout by purchasing Flying Tiger Line, making it the largest all-cargo airline in the world.

The success of Federal Express (the name was changed to FedEx in 1994) led to the establishment of competing airfreight operations, most notably that of

Workers load cargo onto a UPS airplane in Miami, Florida. Airfreight is the fastest way to ship fresh food and important cargo across the country.

United Parcel Service (UPS). Long a successful deliverer of packages by truck, UPS received permission from the U.S. government in 1988 to operate its own freight-delivery airline. UPS Airlines grew so rapidly that by 2001 it ranked as the ninth-largest airline in the United States. UPS now delivers some 2 million air express packages and documents every day.

Federal Express, UPS Airlines, and similar companies revolutionized the airfreight industry and they made life easier and more efficient for Americans in all walks of life. For example, before these companies came into being, a mechanic who needed an automobile part in order to complete repairs on a customer's car would have to wait days to receive the part. Now the part can be delivered in less than 24 hours. A pharmacy suddenly finding itself out of a medicine needed by a customer can confidently expect to have it arrive in the same short period of time.

The services provided by these private companies (and the U.S. Postal Service's Express Mail operations) go beyond the delivery of packages. Even in this age of faxes and e-mail there are printed materials such as contracts, insurance policies, and many other types of business and personal documents that are valid only in their original form. Next-day delivery of these materials makes up a large percentage of the business that FedEx, UPS, and their competitors conduct. Rapid transmittal of vital documents is just one more way in which the airplane has changed the day-to-day lives of people all over the world.

Special Deliveries

Companies such as FedEx and UPS are best known for the millions of small packages they deliver. What fewer people know is that their fleets of jumbo jets have also delivered some unique and huge items. In 1999, for example, a customized Boeing 747 from the UPS fleet, named *Panda Express,* airlifted male and female giant pandas Lun Lun and Yang Yang from Beijing, China, to their new home at Zoo Atlanta in Georgia.

Airlines have transported some other unusual items:

- Keiko, the whale that starred in the movie *Free Willy*

- A railroad locomotive for the Smithsonian Institution

- A full plane-load of live lobsters from Boston to Los Angeles

- A four-ton elephant, two zebras, four monkeys, and several toucans from Ontario, California, to Honolulu, Hawaii, where the animals appeared in the Disney movie *George of the Jungle.*

Keiko, star of the *Free Willy* movies, is loaded by crane into a truck. The 10,000-pound whale was then flown to Iceland and later released into the wild.

CHAPTER 5

Change and Challenge

"It's a magical feeling to climb toward the heavens,
seeing objects and people on the ground grow smaller and more insignificant.
You have left that world beneath you. You are within the sky."

—Pilot and astronaut Gordon Cooper,
in an interview in the *New York Times*, 2000

"Science has not yet mastered prophecy," the astronaut Neil Armstrong said in a speech to space-agency officials in 1971. "We predict too much for the next year and yet far too little for the next ten." It was a perceptive statement. For as the 1970s began, few—not even Armstrong, who only two years earlier had become the first person to walk on the moon—could have foreseen the changes and the challenges that lay ahead for the world of aviation in the three decades to come. Nor could they have predicted the effect these changes and challenges would have on the American people.

One of the most significant developments that took place in this period was the way in which travel by airplane, once an activity for the wealthy, became far more affordable to ordinary citizens. What has been called the "democratization of air travel" began in the 1970s with the formation of People's Express and Southwest airlines, both offering low-cost, no-frills service. So many Americans began taking advantage of the budget prices that many of the larger airlines were forced to reduce their prices on some of their routes in order to stay competitive.

Because of management problems, People's Express was never able to make a profit and was sold to Continental Airlines in 1986. However, Southwest Airlines, which began operations in 1971, has been a true success. Based on the philosophy of one of its founders, Herb Kelleher, that "if you get your passengers to their destinations when they want to get there, on time, at the lowest possible fares, and make darn sure they have a good time doing it, people will fly your airline." Today, Southwest Airlines has become the fourth-largest airline in America. Southwest's 2,700 flights a day to 59 cities in the United States carry more than 64 million passengers a year.

In addition to reducing the cost of flying on many air routes, Southwest has been responsible for several

An airline pilot goes through his preflight check. The computerized navigation system charts the route and then the pilot checks the calculations manually.

other innovations, all of benefit to air travelers. The airline pioneered senior discounts, and it was also the first airline to institute a frequent-flyer program that gave people credit for the number of trips taken rather than for the number of miles flown. Southwest also pioneered electronic ticketing, a convenience that relieved travelers of the burden of standing in long lines at a ticket counter or having to use a travel agent. Many of these innovations have been adopted by other airlines around the world.

Changes in recent decades have also included the appearance of even bigger airliners, which are made possible by continued technological advances. In 1992, for example, Boeing's 767 airliners went into serv-

ice. Featuring engines that provided greater thrust than those of any previous jetliners and a wingspan of more than 170 feet, the 767 was the most sophisticated commercial aircraft ever constructed.

The size of these airplanes and other jumbo jets, along with the ever-increasing amount of air traffic, led to the dramatic alteration of the world's major airports. Runways had to be built much longer to accommodate the long takeoffs and landings of the enormous

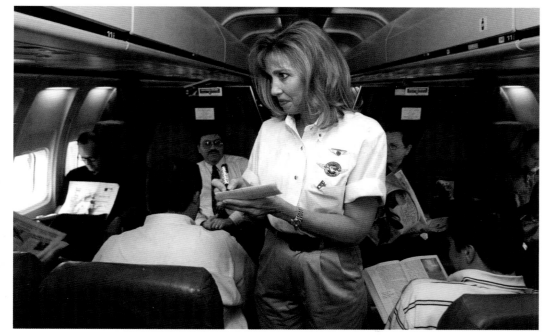

A flight attendant takes meal orders from travelers in business class. In order to keep up with the competition, businesspeople have found that air travel is not only a convenience, but often a necessity.

new aircraft. Many airport terminals have also been redesigned in order to handle the flow of millions of passengers. By 2000, more than one billion people used airports in the United States every year.

Most major airports now have corridors that extend from the central terminal out to what are called "satellites," areas from which many airliners arrive and depart. As airports were enlarged and the distance between the terminal itself and the arrival and departure gates increased significantly, moving sidewalks were installed to enable travelers to cope more easily with these distances.

In order to manage their huge aircraft traffic, some of the larger airports, such as Dulles Airport near Washington, D.C., actually have airliners park a considerable distance away from the terminal. Passengers are transported to and from their airplanes by large bus-like

To reward their steadiest customers and attract repeat business, most major airlines offer free flights or other benefits based on the number of miles or trips customers fly. This Rapid Rewards card is issued to frequent fliers on Southwest Airlines, a pioneer in passenger rewards programs.

vehicles called "people movers." Atlanta's Hartsfield Airport handles so many passengers each year that it moves its travelers to and from their arrival and departure areas on a train that runs through its terminals.

The enormous amount of traffic in America's skies has also necessitated profound changes in the way this traffic is controlled. During commercial aviation's early days, U.S. air traffic control systems used high-frequency radios to aid and coordinate pilot navigation. Pilots reported their positions over the radios, and air traffic controllers responded with maneuvering instructions. When, in 1956, two airliners collided

Passengers wait to board a flight at Logan Airport in Boston, Massachusetts. Serving more than 23 million passengers a year, Logan has its own state police troop, fire-rescue unit, and chapel.

positions of aircraft, the system required crews to file detailed flight plans before their departure, and required both pilots and controllers to maintain direct communication with VHF (very high frequency) radios. Controllers provide regular radio reports to each aircraft, informing pilots of the distances between them and any other planes in the sky nearby.

over the Grand Canyon because of errors in this communication, it became clear that a far more sophisticated air traffic control system was needed.

Radar, which, like the jet engine, had been developed for military purposes during World War II, became the basis of the new air traffic control system. In addition to the use of radar to continually track the

With more than 120 million commercial- and general-aviation flights each year in the United States, the job of air traffic controllers has become more detailed and more challenging than ever. Certain controllers direct each plane during takeoff and landing. Other controllers follow the flight of a plane during each part of its journey, making sure that the flight is proceeding without incident along the route of the filed flight plan. Still other controllers warn pilots about nearby planes, bad weather conditions, and other potential hazards. It is a complex system, one for which aviation authorities continually seek new and more sophisticated equipment and new ways to keep air traffic moving as smoothly and as safely as possible.

Large jetliners and commercial aviation are not the only areas of the field that have seen changes in recent times. The development and increased availability of light, durable materials, including metals, plastics, and

An air traffic controller monitors flights on her computer. Her responsibilities include giving pilots takeoff and landing instructions and making certain that the planes she monitors keep a safe distance from one another.

carbon fibers, have enabled airplane enthusiasts to construct and fly their own craft. Among the most popular of these planes are the so-called ultralights, which are essentially gliders with motors strapped to them—not unlike the Wright brothers' original craft.

Ultralights are used almost exclusively for recreational flying, but the tens of thousands of private propeller- or jet-powered aircraft that fill the nation's skies also play a significant role in transportation. These airplanes—built by aircraft companies such as Lear, Beech, Piper, and Cessna—are used primarily by corporations to transport key personnel and important clients, as well as by wealthy individuals who can afford to fly wherever and whenever they wish.

As is the case with almost all progress, the modern achievements in flight have brought with them new challenges. Most significant were the terrorist attacks of September 11, 2001, during which hijackers crashed passenger airliners into the twin towers of the World Trade Center in New York City, the Pentagon outside Washington, D.C., and a field in Pennsylvania. In addition to the loss of more than 3,000 lives, the attacks had an enormous impact on the world of aviation.

In an attempt to protect against further attacks of this kind, thousands of additional security guards, baggage checkers, and other personnel had to be hired at airports. Special government agents called sky marshals were placed on certain flights for added passenger security. These measures cost the airlines tens of millions of dollars.

Airlines suffered further financial damage when thousands of people, concerned for their safety or unwilling to endure the long lines caused by increased security measures such as the meticulous checking of baggage and other personal items, simply stopped flying. Faced with huge losses in revenue, some airline executives questioned whether such strict security measures were necessary. But as aviation expert Arnold Barnett of the Massachusetts Institute of Technology stated in the 2002 issue of *Aviation Magazine,* "No one in his right mind really wants to have security measures that are [unnecessary], but September 11 did happen and it

President George W. Bush works at his desk aboard *Air Force One*, the official Presidential airplane. Equipped with computers, fax machines, offices, and meeting rooms, *Air Force One* allows American Presidents to carry out important work while traveling to distant destinations.

could happen again." To make matters worse, the attack came at a time when many major airlines were already in financial distress because of a weak economy, the high price of fuel, competition from low-fare "no frills" passenger carriers, and other factors.

Yet, despite these setbacks, most aviation experts and much of the public believed that through consolidation, downsizing, or other means, the airlines would rebound. In fact, many authorities and public officials expected that the airlines' troubled times would force them to eliminate inefficiencies that have long plagued the industry and to adopt long-overdue improvements in their management practices.

Even with security concerns, by 2002, many Americans did return to flying. "The hassles of having myself and my bags checked often more than once are, of course annoying," says Connecticut businessman Jim Nolan. "But I found that I simply could not operate efficiently without using the airlines. Besides, I was, and remain, determined not to let the threat of terrorism change the way I live."

Perhaps the best indication of the confidence that key players in the aviation world have in the future of the industry can be seen in the fact that Boeing, the world's largest manufacturer of airliners, continues to develop even bigger and more sophisticated aircraft. Boeing's latest project is the development of its ultra-long-range 777-200LR airliner. This new jet will seat 301 passengers and will fly more than 9,100 nautical miles for nonstop trips such as Singapore to New York, Dallas to Hong Kong, and Chicago to Sydney, Australia. "We believe that there is a strong market for the 777-200LR," said Lars Andersen in a 2002 speech to company stockholders, Boeing's 777 Longer Range program manager. "As the world's economy improves and travel growth returns, we're convinced that we'll see [increasing] sales." It is a confidence typical of those who continue to make airplanes an indispensable part of our lives.

Timeline

1900
Wilbur and Orville Wright begin testing gliders near Kitty Hawk, North Carolina

1901
Samuel Pierpont Langley flies quarter-scale gasoline-powered model airplane

1903
Langley launches full-size gasoline-powered airplane, which crashes on takeoff; Wilbur and Orville Wright accomplish first manned, powered flight

1918
First airmail flight in the United States

1919
John Alcock and Arthur Whitten Brown complete successful flight from Newfoundland to Ireland

1921
Airmail is flown from San Francisco to New York City for the first time

1927
Charles Lindbergh completes the first solo flight across the Atlantic Ocean

1928
National Air Pilots Association is formed

1929
Pan American Airways begins passenger service

1930
Ellen Church becomes the first airline stewardess

1932
Amelia Earhart becomes the first woman to fly solo across the Atlantic

1933
Wiley Post becomes the first person to fly solo around the world

1945–1950
The jet engine is developed

1946
Flying Tiger airfreight line is established

1947
Chuck Yeager becomes the first human to fly faster than the speed of sound; Marion J. Carl sets altitude record of 82,235 feet

1969
Boeing introduces the first wide-body jet, the 747

1970
Airbus introduces its first wide-body jet

1971
Southwest Airlines begins operations

1973
Federal Express begins service

1988
UPS Airlines begins operations

1992
Boeing introduces its 767 jumbo jet

2001
Hijacked airliners are deliberately crashed into the World Trade Center and the Pentagon

Places to Visit

The following museums display aircraft from almost every era of flight. Most also feature films and photographic exhibits chronicling the history of the airplane in the United States.

Alabama

Southern Museum of Flight
4343 73rd Street North
Birmingham, AL 35206-3642
205-833-8226
www.southernmuseumofflight.org

California

Museum of Flying
2772 Donald Douglas Loop North
Santa Monica, CA 90405
310-392-8822
www.museumofflying.com

District of Columbia

National Air & Space Museum
7th and Independence Avenue, SW
Washington, DC 20560
202-357-2700
www.nasm.si.edu

Illinois

Air Classics Museum
Aurora Municipal Airport
43W776 U.S. Route 30
Sugar Grove, IL 60554
630-466-0888
www.airclassicsmuseum.org

Michigan

Henry Ford Museum
20900 Oakwood Boulevard
Dearborn, MI 48124
313-982-6100
www.thehenryford.org/museum/heroes

New Jersey

New Jersey Aviation Hall of Fame
    and Museum
400 Fred Wehran Drive
Teterboro, NJ 07608
201-288-6344
www.njahof.org

New York

Cradle of Aviation Museum
Charles Lindbergh Boulevard
Garden City, NY 11530
516-572-4111
www.cradleofaviation.org

North Carolina

Wright Brothers National Memorial
1401 National Park Drive
Manteo, NC 27954
252-441-7430
www.nps.gov/wrbr/index.htm

Ohio

National Aviation Hall of Fame
1100 Spaatz Street
Wright Patterson Air Force Base
Dayton, OH 45433
937-256-0944
www.nationalaviation.org

Texas

Frontiers of Flight Museum
Love Field Terminal, Upper Level
Dallas, TX 75235
214-350-1651
http://flightmuseum.com

Washington

Museum of Flight
9404 East Marginal Way South
Seattle, WA 98108
206-764-5700
www.museumofflight.org

Further Reading

Boyne, Walter. *The Smithsonian Book of Flight.* New York: Wings Books, 1994.

Briggs, Carole. *At the Controls: Women in Aviation.* Minneapolis: Lerner, 1991.

Butler, Susan. *East to the Dawn: The Life of Amelia Earhart.* New York: Da Capo, 1999.

Crouch, Tom D., and Peter L. Jakab. *The Wright Brothers and the Invention of the Aerial Age.* Washington D.C.: National Geographic Society, 2003.

————. *Wings: A History of Aviation from Kites to the Space Age.* Washington, D.C.: Smithsonian National Air and Space Museum, 2003.

Davidson, Marshall B. *Life in America.* Boston: Houghton Mifflin, 1974.

Dunsmore, Spencer, Fred Culick, and Peter Christopher. *On Great Wings: The Wright Brothers and the Race for Flight.* New York: Hyperion, 2001.

Gandt, Robert L. *China Clipper: The Age of the Great Flying Boats.* Annapolis, Md.: Naval Institute Press, 1991.

Heppenheimer, T. A. *A Brief History of Flight: From Balloons to Mach 3 and Beyond.* New York: Wiley, 2001.

Lindbergh, Charles. *The Spirit of St. Louis.* New York: Scribner, 1998.

Lopez, Donald. *Flight.* Alexandria, Va.: Time-Life Books, 1995.

McLoone, Margo, and Jacqueline Bever. *Women Explorers of the Air.* Mankato, Minn.: Capstone, 2000.

Nevin, David. *The Pathfinders.* Alexandria, Va.: Time-Life Books, 1980.

Nicolaou, Stèphane. *Flying Boats and Seaplanes: A History from 1905.* Osceola, Wisc.: Motorbooks, 1998.

Ott, James, and Aram Gesar. *Jets: Airliners of the Golden Age.* Osceola, Wisc.: Motorbooks, 1993.

Payne, Lee. *Lighter Than Air: An Illustrated History of the Airship.* Rev. ed. New York: Orion, 1991.

Sarling, Robert. *The Jet Age.* Alexandria, Va.: Time-Life Books, 1982.

Williamson, Katherine S. *The Golden Age of Aviation.* New York: Smithmark, 1996.

Wright, Orville. *How We Invented the Airplane: An Illustrated History.* New York: Dover, 1988.

Yeager, Chuck, and Leo Janos. *Yeager: An Autobiography.* New York: Bantam, 1985.

Index

References to illustrations are indicated by page numbers in **bold**.

Acknowledgments

I wish to thank Carol Sandler and Karen Fein for their valuable assistance. I am also indebted to Katherine Williams and Mike McMillan for their generous assistance. Finally, I am particularly grateful for having Nancy Hirsch as my editor. Her editing skills are but part of the many contributions she has made to this book.

Picture Credits

Federal Aviation Administration: 53; The Hawk Eye: 42; Library of Congress: 7, 14, 15, 20, 25, 31; Mike McMillan/Spotfire Images: 39, 40; Museum of Flight: 29, 35; NASA: 10; Jack Naylor Collection: 22; NOAA/Department of Commerce, Mrs. Marge Beaver, Photography Plus: 43; NOAA/Department of Commerce, Captain Budd Christman, NOAA Corps: 37; Sandler Collection: 52; Smithsonian National Air and Space Museum: 9, 13, 16, 18, 24, 26, 28, 30, 36; Courtesy of Southwest Airlines: 50, 51; Courtesy of Richard Stevens: 49; U.S. Air Force: 33; U.S. Department of Defense: 47; Courtesy of UPS: 45; The White House: 55; Western Reserve Historical Society, Cleveland Ohio: cover, frontispiece

Martin W. Sandler is the author of more than 40 books. His *Story of American Photography: An Illustrated History for Young People* received the Horn Book Award in 1984. Sandler's other books include *America, A Celebration!, Photography: An Illustrated History, The Vaqueros: The World's First Cowmen,* and the Library of Congress American history series for young adults. An accomplished television producer and writer as well, Sandler has received Emmy and Golden Cine awards for his television series and programs on history, photography, and American business. He has taught American studies to students in junior high and high school, as well as at the University of Massachusetts and Smith College. He lives in Cotuit, Massachusetts, with his wife, Carol.

Other titles in the Transportation in America series include:

Galloping across the USA: Horses in American Life

On the Waters of the USA: Ships and Boats in American Life

Straphanging in the USA: Trolleys and Subways in American Life

Riding the Rails in the USA: Trains in American Life

Driving around the USA: Automobiles in American Life